What's Your Style?

BOHO
FASHION

KAREN LATCHANA KENNEY

Lerner Publications Company
Minneapolis

Lerner Publications Company
A division of Lerner Publishing Group, Inc.
241 First Avenue North
Minneapolis, MN 55401 U.S.A.

For reading levels and more information,
lookup this title at www.lernerbooks.com

Credits: Sara E. Hoffmann (editorial), Emily Harris (design),
Giliane Mansfeldt (photos), Heidi Hogg (production).

Main body text set in Adrianna Light 12/14.
Typeface provided by Chank.

Library of Congress Cataloging-in-Publication Data

Kenney, Karen Latchana.
    Boho fashion / by Karen Latchana Kenney ; illustrated by Ashley
  Newsome Kubley
      pages   cm. — (What's your style?)
    Includes index.
    ISBN 978–1–4677–1470–9 (library binding)
    ISBN 978–1–4677–2526–2 (eBook)
    1. Fashion—Juvenile literature. 2. Girls' clothing—Juvenile literature.
  3. Bohemianism—Juvenile literature. I. Kubley, Ashley Newsome—ill. II. Title.
  TT507.K4168 2014
  746.9'2—dc23   2013011590

Manufactured in the United States of America
1 – PC – 12/31/13

What's Your Style?

Are *You* BOHO?

Do you love fashion? Is the flowy, feminine boho look for you? Take this quiz to find out if you're a boho girl!

1. What was the best decade for fashion?
   a. 1920s
   b. 1980s
   c. 1960s
   d. 1990s

2. Which celeb has the best style?
   a. Selena Gomez
   b. Rihanna
   c. Vanessa Hudgens
   d. Beyoncé

3. Your favorite earrings are
   a. diamond studs
   b. hot pink and sparkly
   c. long, beaded, and dangly
   d. shaped like lightning bolts

4. What kinds of colors do you love to wear?
   a. bold neon
   b. pretty pastels
   c. earthy and warm
   d. all black

5. You never leave the house without your
   a. glittery boots
   b. black-rimmed glasses
   c. fringed purse
   d. vintage sneakers

6. If you had to describe your personality in one word, you'd pick
   a. classic
   b. boyish
   c. eclectic
   d. glamorous

Did you answer mostly *c*'s? If so, you're **boho chic!** You're all about the laid-back, earthy, and eclectic look.

If you didn't come up with *c*'s, boho might not be your thing. But any fashionista can benefit from learning about different looks. **Keep reading** to discover all the ins and outs of boho style.

Who's Got
THE LOOK?

A great way to learn about any style is to check out those who love to sport it. Lots of celebrities are experts at dressing boho chic. They've got the whole look down—from the long, wavy hair to the best fringed boots. These celebs make boho fashion look effortless and super stylish.

Who are some of the best-dressed boho stars on the scene? We'd be remiss if we didn't start with . . .

VANESSA HUDGENS

This *High School Musical* star is the queen of boho style. Boho lovers everywhere look to her for inspiration. In a 2013 interview, Vanessa explained,

> "I'm a total gypsy bohemian. If I could go back in time, I'd be front row for Janis Joplin at Woodstock."

How does Vanessa get her perfect boho look?
This famous fashionista

- wears tons of loose and flowy pieces;

- isn't afraid to mix it up with fitted clothing—structured camis and fitted leggings add eclectic flair and suit her petite frame;

- wears platforms and flat sandals;

- likes plenty of soft fabrics in earthy colors and prints; and

- adds touches of sparkly jewelry or accessories.

Here's Vanessa wearing some of her boho best.

Make a Lookbook

Look through fashion magazines and celeb photos to find boho looks that you love. Cut the photos out and keep them in a notebook. This is your very own lookbook. Take it with you shopping or when browsing through your closet. Study the outfits in your lookbook. It will help you find the right pieces to pull together for your own great boho style.

Who else is a pro at pulling off boho fashion?

Look no further than these stylish superstar twins.

The two former child stars have become huge names in the fashion world. They have a boho-chic style that's all their own. These girls love anything vintage and visually interesting. When they're out and about, they often

- wear skinny jeans or short shorts with fringy tops;

- sport oversized jackets or big, bell-shaped sleeves;

- accessorize with lots of unusual bracelets and rings;

- wear interesting textures and lots of bold, playful patterns;

- rock super-dark aviator sunglasses; and

- layer with loose sweaters over long skirts.

The next time you've checking out a fashion mag, look for Mary-Kate (right) and Ashley (left) wearing striking styles like the ones they've sporting here.

Mary-Kate and Ashley aren't the only famous faces in boho fashion circles.

Take this next fashionista, for example.

SIENNA MILLER

This British actress has been rocking the boho look for a long time. In fact, she was one of the first celebs to make boho chic really popular.

Sienna loves to

- mix vintage and new pieces in her outfits;

- use funky jewelry to add personality;

- wear oversized sunglasses; and

- add beaded necklaces and stylish hats to top off her look.

Check out some of Sienna's stylish ensembles here.

Who else is known for being boho chic?

It's one of the best-known former reality stars and current TV personalities out there. She's even known for lending fashion advice as a celebrity mentor on the NBC show *Fashion Star.*

NICOLE RICHIE

Nicole's trademark is her big sunglasses.

Boho chic is Nicole's signature style. Casual, loose, and quirky is what Nicole is all about. Look for Nicole wearing cutoffs and flyaway cardis, floppy, fun felt hats, and cute yet comfy maxi dresses.

Nicole also

- loves sequined headbands worn low on her forehead;

- wears pretty prints;

- layers shorts, tights, and boots; and, like many boho girls;

- can't get enough of those big, dark sunglasses.

Here, Nicole works boho chic in a pretty fabulous way.

Check Out These Other
Boho Celebs!

KATE HUDSON

Kate looks stylish in this boho maxi dress.

RACHEL ZOE

An oversized floppy hat completes Rachel's boho look.

KATE MOSS

Kate's fringy vest is boho chic.

How Do I
GET THE LOOK?

Before you start creating flawless boho outfits, you have to learn a few basics. What colors are boho-friendly? And what kinds of patterns and fabrics should you choose? There are some simple guidelines you can follow. Take a look at these tips before you gather your boho-chic wardrobe.

Earthy Colors

When choosing which colors to add to your closet, look to nature for inspiration. Think brown, gray, black, gold, deep green, khaki, and cream. Of course, nature also includes pops of color—and so should your wardrobe! Turquoise blue jewelry or a coral scarf can add to your look, just as bright wildflowers add to the beauty of a woodsy landscape.

NATURAL TEXTURES AND FABRICS

When it comes to fabrics, you'll want to stay away from polyester and plastic. Instead, use natural materials for your boho outfits. Wood bracelets and beads, leather bags, and straw hats are good choices. Cotton and wool are great too. Feathers make awesome accents for jewelry or your hair. And anything crocheted, embroidered, or woven is always a safe bet.

Boho-Chic Influences

The boho look has lots of different influences. But many parts of it come from the beat and hippie movements of the 1950s and the 1960s. These were artistic movements focused on freedom and individuality. People who embraced beat and hippie lifestyles often wore peasant- and gypsy-style clothing. They sported different patterns, vintage pieces, and modern finds all in one outfit. This earthy, eclectic, and relaxed-yet-put-together look has come to define boho style today.

Janis Joplin—a 1960s music and fashion icon

Pretty Prints

A boho girl looks a bit like a world traveler. She wears bracelets from India and African-printed skirts. Beautiful Moroccan sandals and earrings and printed Japanese kimonos are also often a part of her look. When crafting your own boho style, you can try all of these pieces and more. Also keep an eye out for patterns, such as floral and paisley prints on dresses, blouses, skirts, and scarves.

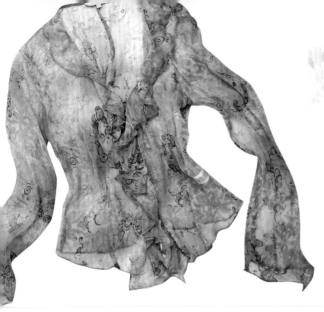

CLOTHING

Now that you have a few key guidelines under your belt, let's go even more in-depth and take a close look at clothing. Exactly what kinds of clothes will you need to pull off boho? Just a handful of must-have pieces will get you there.

PEASANT BLOUSE

A peasant blouse is a defining boho garment. These loose, flowing blouses often have bell-shaped arms, open or ruffled bottoms, and lace, embroidery, or other pretty details. Lots of stores, from discount shops to pricey boutiques, carry this type of top. Thrift stores are also great places to check. They often have one-of-a-kind pieces to help set you apart from the crowd.

The Croatian TV program Fashion Week Zagreb features models sporting boho maxi dresses in 2011.

Alexandra Burke shows off a super cute maxi at the 2011 Glamour Awards.

Maxi Dress or Long Skirt

All true boho girls have one or more of these in their closets. Maxi dresses are simply long, feminine dresses that often reach all the way to the floor. Long skirts are good alternatives if maxi dresses aren't your thing. You can find them almost anywhere, in all kinds of fun colors, patterns, and styles.

Drapey, Long Cardigan

Cardis are cute layering pieces to add to your boho wardrobe. Think delicate knits and bold, pretty prints when choosing a cardigan of your own. Lots of boho cardigans have ties so you can cinch them to add a little structure. Or pair them with a belt to pull off the same look. That will help keep you from drowning in a sea of flowing fabric! Picking cardigan colors and patterns that you love is a great way to add your own special flair.

Torn, Faded Denim

You might already have some of this in your closet. If so, you can check it off your list! Any distressed (read: worn-looking) denim piece will do, from jeans to cutoffs to a vintage denim jacket. You can even create a distressed look in new denim by snipping a hole or two in it with a scissors. Just be sure to check with a parent before breaking out the scissors! Not all moms and dads will be okay with you doing your own version of tailoring on new clothes.

MIX & MATCH

Now you know which pieces are boho musts. But you can't wear all boho, all the time. You need to mix more traditional pieces with modern pieces to be boho chic. It's also smart to mix fitted pieces with flowy pieces. And your colors should be balanced too. Here are a few tips for getting a good boho mix:

- To avoid going overboard with the flowy look, don't wear loose clothing from head to toe. Balance a fitted top with a loose skirt. Or wear a long tunic with skinny jeans.

- Avoid wearing only patterned clothing. Mix bold prints with solids. For example, try a solid-color cardigan over a pretty floral top.

This goes great with skinny jeans.

An adorable pairing!

Wear this with a fitted top.

- For most of your outfit, try to stay in the same color family—but then add pops of accent colors. Use a mix of three to four colors total.

- Think outside the box when deciding which items to wear together. That cute vintage dress you found at the thrift shop just might go perfectly over the brand-new patterned leggings you scored at the department store.

Now you've got all the clothing, and you know how to wear it. What's even more fun than picking out boho clothes? Just one thing: shoe shopping! Lucky for you, that's our very next stop.

vintage sweaters add character to newer finds.

A colorful blouse complements earth tones.

Thrift-shop skirt + department-store leggings = fun!

Styling DIY:

Boho Thrifting

On a tight budget? Or looking to shop in a way that's friendly to the environment? If either of these are the case, you can re-create your favorite boho look from only thrift store finds. It's fun to do, and it's pretty easy too. Here are some steps to help you out:

1. First, find a boho look in a magazine and cut it out. Bring the image to your local thrift store.

2. Look in the plus-size area to find dresses and skirts. Plus-sized items will have the volume needed for boho looks. Find a similar pattern or similar colors as the outfit in the image.

Look for boho staples (like paisley prints and fringes) at thrift stores.

3. Find a top that has colors that match the skirt or the dress. Look for interesting details, such as embroidery, lace, and crocheted elements.

4. Look for shoes in an earthy color and natural-looking material. Choose sandals, booties (short boots), or regular-length boots.

5. Try the men's area for hats and suit jackets. You can find a great fedora or a blazerlike jacket.

6. Need an oversized purse? Try the luggage area and look for the smaller luggage pieces. They are usually less popular than bigger pieces of luggage. And they can look just like purses.

Try everything on, and remember that you can mix your thrift store finds with what you have at home.

SHOES

Just like your clothes, you want your shoes to have that natural and earthy vibe. Leather, wood, and cork are great boho shoe materials. And like every other part of your outfit, make sure your shoes are in balance with what you're wearing. Let's check out the different types of shoes that define boho.

This model's look is from the Michael Kors Spring/Summer 2012 collection at Mercedes-Benz Fashion Week.

STRAPPY SANDALS

Funky sandals are perfect for boho fashion. Leather gladiators add a simple touch. Beaded sandals are colorful and have great texture. Fringe and tassels make nice touches too. You can choose either heels or flats—both work well for the boho look.

Boots
and Booties

Tall boots are really comfortable and can be worn over leggings and jeans. They also look great with skirts and dresses. Look for boots in suede or leather. Find ones with interesting details. Buckles and straps, tassels and fringe, and slouchy sides make for fantastic boho boots. Traditional cowboy boots work well too. And choose from heels, wedges, or flats—all fit the style.

Booties add a modern twist. Find the same details you'd look for in boots. When you wear them, try adding some long, eclectic socks. You can also try wearing two pairs of socks for a cute layered look.

Booties are a fun accompaniment to almost any look.

Flats
and Moccasins

Flats come in all kinds of patterns and colors. Look for ones that have beading or embroidery. You can also find woven or canvas flats. And moccasins have a nice natural look. As an extra plus, many moccasins have fringe and pretty beaded details.

Sandal Restyle

You can make your own colorful gladiator sandals from basic flip-flops.

What you need:

- scissors

- a long, thin piece of pretty patterned material (3 to 4 feet [0.9 to 1.2 meters] long and 10 to 12 inches [25 to 30 centimeters] wide)

- flip-flops

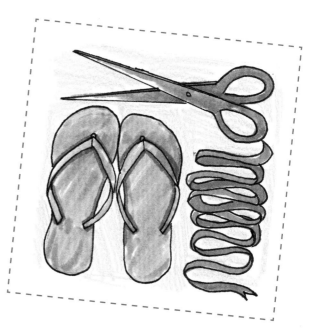

What you do:

1. Cut your material in half, making two equally long strips.

2. Fold one piece of one strip in half. Now the folded end makes a loop. The loose ends are together.

3. Put the folded loop around the thong (toe-divider) part of your flip-flop.

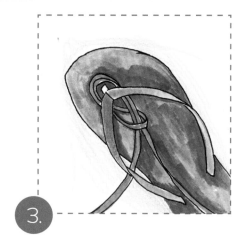

4. Fold the loose ends of the strip over the thong and through the folded loop. Pull the strip tight around the thong.

5. You have two ends of the strip coming up from the thong now. Wrap each piece around the straps of the flip-flops. Keep wrapping until the straps cannot be seen.

6. Once the straps are covered, it's time to tie your sandals onto your ankles. Put your foot in and wrap the strip pieces behind your ankle.

7. Pull the pieces forward to the front of your ankle. Wrap them around your ankle a few more times. Then tie the strip of cloth in a knot, letting the ends dangle down.

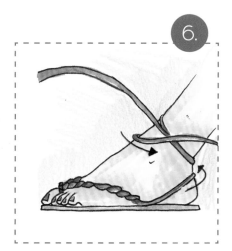

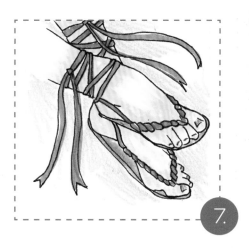

ACCESSORIES

Finding boho accessories is right up there with shoe shopping on the fun scale! After all, you can really change up a look with accessories. And the boho look is all about jewelry, scarves, hats, headbands, belts, and bags.

How you use accessories can show your personal boho style. Take a look at the different ways you can accessorize your boho outfit.

Beaded necklaces are a boho must-have item.

BRACELETS AND NECKLACES

A model shows off boho style at Miami Fashion Week.

These add a ton of personality to your look. Think beaded, chunky, and big—and don't forget your layers! This is where you can really play with your outfit. Put several bracelets on and mix beaded, wood, and metal. Add thin beaded and leather bracelets and large cuffs.

Long pendant necklaces look great around your neck. Wear a few at a time. Or add a colorful shorter and chunky necklace. It's an awesome way to add a pop of color. Long necklaces can also be worn as bracelets. Just wind them around your wrists a few times.

Beautiful bangles add pizzazz to an outfit.

CHUNKY RINGS

Big rings make a big statement. Look for ones with stones and bright colors. A turquoise stone works well with boho outfits. Try wearing several rings at a time for extra style.

DANGLY EARRINGS

Long, beaded, and dangly earrings pair perfectly with boho clothing. They add a carefree but dressy vibe. Hammered metal earrings look great too. And if your earrings have feathers, that's even better!

BOHO HEADBANDS

Boho headbands are taken straight out of the 1970s. Think flower child! These headbands are worn low on the forehead. Go casual with a braided headband. Dress it up with a silver or gold chain headband.

FLIRTY SCARVES

When it comes to scarves, think thin and filmy with a bit of fringe and pattern. They're versatile and add pretty pops of color and texture. Tie one in a loose knot around your neck. Wrap one around your head for a real gypsy look. Or use one as a pretty belt around your jeans or skirt.

Fun Hats

A hat makes a cool and casual boho accessory. And almost any hat fits in with the style. Try a structured fedora. An oversized floppy hat is ideal for sunny days. A warm, slouchy beanie is a good bet for colder days. Look for natural materials, such as straw, wool, or cotton.

Boho Bags

Certain styles of bags are more boho than others. For example, try a suede or leather hobo with some long fringe. Messenger cross-body bags have a casual vibe. Slouchy bags look a bit rough and carefree. And clutches work well for dressier looks. Try to find clutches that are beaded or have a pretty woven pattern.

BIG BELTS

Most boho tops and dresses are big and flowy. To highlight your waist, use a big or skinny belt. A belt gives those loose shapes more definition. Find leather belts with metal accents or a braided design. Beadwork can look beautiful on belts. And remember, you can use scarves as belts too!

OVERSIZED SUNGLASSES

When it comes to sunglasses, the bigger you go, the better! Aim for that bug-eyed look! Or try a large aviator style.

Styling DIY:

Boho Headband

Do you have an old necklace lying around? You can turn it into a glitzy boho headband.

What you need:

- a necklace that is 14 to 17 inches (35.5 to 43.1 cm) long

- a pencil or tape

- a no-slip elastic headband in a matching color

- a ruler

- scissors

- a needle

- thread in a matching color

What you do:

1. Unclasp the necklace and lay it on your head. Position it so that the ends fall behind your ears.

2. Holding the necklace in place on your head (you may need a friend to help you here!), position the headband behind your head so that one end of it is touching each end of the necklace. The idea is to see how long the headband needs to be to connect to the necklace. It is what will hold the necklace securely on your head.

3. Once you've figured out how long the headband needs to be, mark the length on the headband with a pencil or some tape.

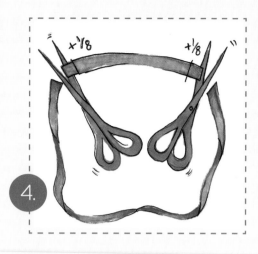

4. Measure 1/8 inch (3.2 millimeters) from the spots you've marked on each side of the headband. Then cut the headband at the exact spots you've measured.

5. Fold over each end of the headband by 1/8 inch (3.2 mm). Use the needle and thread to sew the ends in place. This stops the headband from fraying.

6. Finally, stitch 1/2 inch (12.7 mm) of the elastic to each end of the necklace. Make sure to fold the clasp under the elastic before you sew. This hides the clasp and makes a clean line. Use 10 to 12 stitches on each side of the headband.

7. Your boho headband is done. Just slip it around your head for a cute look!

Hair and Makeup

Once your clothes, shoes, and accessories are set to go, it's time to turn to hair and makeup. A boho girl should look natural and never overdone. Heavy makeup and severe hairstyles just won't do. You want to have a fresh-looking face and free-looking hair. Check out these hair and makeup ideas to complete your boho look.

Glowing Skin

Before you start applying color, you'll want to make sure you have dewy skin. Instead of heavy foundation, try a tinted cream or a mineral powder. These give more of a natural look. Find one with broad-spectrum SPF to protect your skin from the sun. On top of your cream or powder, add a bit of gel or cream blush or a bronzer for a healthful glow.

Natural Eyes and Lips

Use natural shadow colors on your eyes—think golds, browns, and peaches. Soft eyeliner and mascara define the eyes. Then add a touch of peachy gloss to your lips. Your boho-style makeup is done!

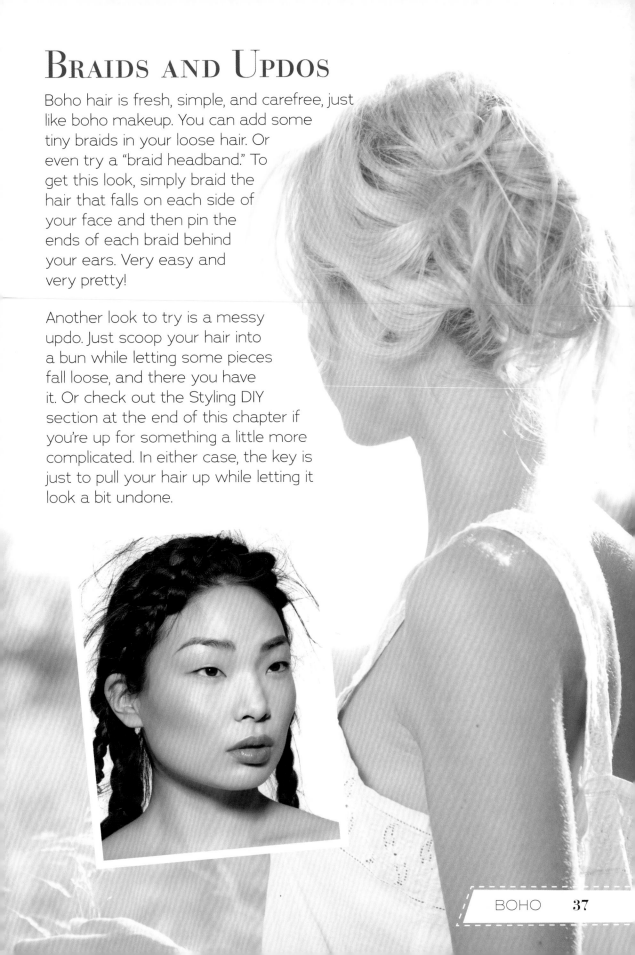

Braids and Updos

Boho hair is fresh, simple, and carefree, just like boho makeup. You can add some tiny braids in your loose hair. Or even try a "braid headband." To get this look, simply braid the hair that falls on each side of your face and then pin the ends of each braid behind your ears. Very easy and very pretty!

Another look to try is a messy updo. Just scoop your hair into a bun while letting some pieces fall loose, and there you have it. Or check out the Styling DIY section at the end of this chapter if you're up for something a little more complicated. In either case, the key is just to pull your hair up while letting it look a bit undone.

BEACHY WAVES

If braids and updos aren't your thing, you can go for something even more free and loose. It's beachy waves! These are simply long, flowing waves that make it look as though you just stepped off the beach. It does take a few steps to get this look, though—and it may not work with all hair types. For example, if your hair is very coarse or very fine, beachy waves might not be for you. If your hair is of medium thickness, though, listen up! And grab some styling spray, because you're going to need it.

The first step to getting beachy waves is to wash your hair. Then twist it up while it's still wet, pin it, and let it dry that way. Next, take the hairpins out and gently comb through your hair to get rid of any snarls. If your hair still isn't as wavy as you'd like, use a curling iron to make it wavier. Finally, apply the styling spray, and you're set to go!

Fun Feathers

Another fun boho look is feathered hair clip-ins. These mimic hair extensions, but they don't require a pricey trip to the salon. Just visit a beauty supply store or a discount store and find some feather hair clip-ins. Clip them on, and you're all set! Or you could opt for a great feathered headband instead. If you can't find one in stores, you can make your own with a headband, feathers from an arts and crafts store, and a little bit of glue.

Styling DIY:

Messy Updo

This updo uses a scarf to pull the look together.

What you need:

- a thin, colorful scarf

- two ponytail holders

What you do:

1. Pull your bangs (if you have them) or the part of your hair that is nearest your face into a small ponytail. The idea is to get this hair out of the way for the moment. Then part the rest of your hair down the middle.

2. Roll or fold the scarf into a long, thin piece. Place the scarf just behind the part of your hair that is in the small ponytail.

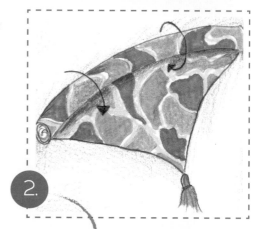

3. Pull the two ends of the scarf to the back of your head. Leave them untied. Then use a ponytail holder to pull both your hair and the scarf into a ponytail at the nape of your neck.

4. Grab the two ends of the scarf and separate them, along with your hair in the ponytail.

5. Twist one end of the scarf into one half of your ponytail. Then twist the other end of the scarf into the other half of your ponytail.

6. Tuck the end of each half of your ponytail into the ponytail holder at the nape of your neck to make a bun.

7. Take the front part of your hair out of the ponytail holder. Let it fall loose around your face.

8. Tuck a few pieces of hair back around the scarf to finish the style. Looks carefree and cute, doesn't it?

Your BOHO Look

Being boho chic is all about showing your individuality and artistic side. It's great to know the basics and the elements involved with the look. But how you use those elements is up to you!

What kind of boho-chic look will you create? Will you be a classic boho girl? Or maybe the gypsy or hippie look is more your style. That's the fun of fashion. You make it your own. And there's no end to the eclectic looks you can come up with. What will your look be today? Have fun finding out!

A stylish hat adds a classic touch to any boho ensemble.

Loose garments with playful prints will give you a hippie look.

Touches of turquoise in jewelry or clothing bring a gypsy vibe to your wardrobe.

BOHO-CHIC RESOURCES

Do you want to learn more about being boho chic? Check out these ideas.

Where to Find Boho Goodies

- Try craft and fabric stores for beads, feathers, and fabrics.

- Look in vintage and thrift stores for authentic pieces from the 1960s.

- Visit outlet stores for scarves and maxi dresses.

- Go to Indian, African, and Asian stores for clothing with great patterns and unique jewelry.

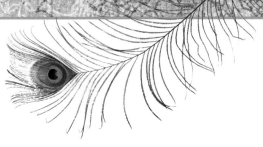

Where to Find Boho Tutorials and Classes

- Look for hair, makeup, and clothing tutorials on YouTube.

- Take a jewelry-making class at a community center to create your own silver, gold, or beaded jewelry.

- Read crafting blogs to find ways to make bags, jewelry, and other boho accessories.

What Songs to Tune into to Inspire Your Inner Boho

- "San Francisco (Be Sure to Wear Some Flowers in Your Hair)" by Scott McKenzie

- "Chicago" by Sufjan Stevens

- "New Slang" by the Shins

- "Summertime" by Janis Joplin and Big Brother & the Holding Company

GLOSSARY

beat: a word to describe a social movement in the 1950s and the early 1960s that stressed artistic self-expression and the rejection of traditional values

booties: short boots

broad-spectrum: a word to describe a sunscreen that protects the skin from both sunburn and skin cancer—two conditions that can develop from too much sun exposure

distressed: worn, or old-looking

eclectic: a word to describe a person or a thing that draws from many different sources. For example, a person with an eclectic fashion sense might draw his or her sense of style from several different time periods or cultures.

fedora: a low, soft felt hat with the crown creased lengthwise

hippie: a person who rejects traditional values and who is against violence and war, or a word to describe the movement that advanced these ideals

kimono: a long robe with wide sleeves traditionally worn in Japan

paisley: printed with colorful curved figures

tunic: a slip-on garment that is typically long and made with or without sleeves

vintage: from the past

SOURCE NOTE

7. Margaret Eby, "Vanessa Hudgens Shows Off Her Inner Flower Child: 'I'm a Total Gypsy Bohemian,'" *New York Daily News*, March 1, 2013, http://www.nydailynews.com/entertainment/gossip/vanessa -hudgens-boho-cosmo-article-1.1277330.

Further Information

Boho Fashions for Fall
http://www.seventeen.com/fashion/tips/boho-fashions-for-fall#slide-1
Visit this website for *Seventeen's* gallery of boho-chic clothing.

Get the Bohemian Chic Look
http://kidsfashion.about.com/od/hotstyles/a/bohemian.htm
Check out this site for advice on getting the boho-chic look.

Niven, Felicia Lowenstein. *Fabulous Fashions of the 1960s*. Berkeley Heights, NJ: Enslow, 2012.
This title tells all about fashions of the 1960s—a decade that inspired the modern boho look.

Shoket, Ann. *Seventeen Ultimate Guide to Style: How to Find Your Perfect Look*. Philadelphia: Running Press, 2011.
Not sure if boho or another style is best for you? Then look to this helpful book to guide you!

Thomas, Isabel. *Being a Fashion Stylist*. Minneapolis: Lerner Publications Company, 2013.
Ever wondered what it's like to work as a fashion stylist? This book is the perfect find for aspiring fashionistas!

Walker, Jackie. *Expressionista: How to Express Your True Self Through (and Despite) Fashion*. New York: Aladdin, 2013.
This title will help you discover your fashion persona and set up a closet to reflect your sense of style.

Index

Photo Acknowlegments

The images in this book are used with the permission of: © Yusuf Doganay/Shutterstock.com, p. 3; © Anton Oparin/Shutterstock.com, pp. 4 (bottom); 29 (bottom left); 32 (bottom left); 42 (right), 43 (top left); © Fibobjects/ Dreamstime.com, p. 4 (top); © Khz/Dreamstime.com, pp. 5 (bottom left), 45 (bottom); © Vnlit/Dreamstime.com, p. 5 (bottom right); © iStockphoto.com/ollo, pp. 5 (top left), 45 (top); © Lisa Maree Williams/Stringer/Getty Images, p. 5 (top right); © Ethan Miller/Getty Images for Pure Nightclub, p. 6; © Jason Merritt/Getty Images for Cirque du Soleil, pp. 7 (right), 10 (top); © Janet Pellegrini/Film Magic/Getty Images, p. 7 (right); © catwalker/Shutterstock.com, pp. 8 (right), 23 (top left), 42 (left), 43 (top right); © Antonio de Moraes Barros Filho/Wire Images/Getty Images, pp. 8 (left), 17 (bottom); © Randy Brooke/WireImage/Getty Images, p. 9 (top); Mario Anzuoni/Splash News/ Newscom, p. 9 (bottom); © Danny Martindale/WireImage/Getty Images, p. 10 (bottom left); © Nick Harvey/ WireImage/Getty Images, p. 10 (bottom center); © Dave Hogan/Getty Images, p. 10 (bottom right); © Jesse Grant/ WireImage/Getty Images, p. 11; © Ray Tamarra/Getty Images, p. 12 (top); © Jeff Vespa/WireImage/Getty Images, p. 12 (bottom); © James Devaney/WireImage/Getty Images, p. 13 (top); © Jason LaVeris/FilmMagic/Getty Images, p. 13 (middle); © Dave M. Benett/Getty Images for Samsung NX Smart Cameras, p. 13 (bottom); © iStockphoto.com/ Jacob Wackerhausen, p. 14; © Michael Ochs/Stringer/Getty Images, p. 15 (bottom); © ppart/Shutterstock.com, p. 15 (top right); © iStockphoto.com/anniam, p. 15 (top left); © iStockphoto.com/mschowe, p. 15 (middle); © Evaletova/Dreamstime.com, pp. 16 (top left), 19 (middle right top), 20 (right bottom), 21 (right); © Manera/Bigstock. com, p. 16 (top middle); © Cristi180884/Bigstock.com, p. 16 (bottom left); © Karkas/Bigstock.com, pp. 16 (bottom right), 17 (top), 17 (middle), 21 (left), 23 (top right); © Natalya Korolevskaya/Dreamstime.com, p. 16 (top right); © Featureflash/Shutterstock.com, p. 18 (bottom); © Gordana/Bigstock.com, p. 18 (top); © iStockphoto/Thinkstock, pp. 19 (bottom right), 19 (middle right bottom), 19 (bottom left), 32 (middle right), 33 (top), 33 (middle); © iStockphoto. com/penguenstok, p. 19 (top left); © iStockphoto.com/Ersinkisacik, p. 19 (middle left); © RuslanOmega/Bigstock. com, pp. 20 (left), 24 (bottom right), 30 (bottom middle), 30 (bottom right); © Ruth Black/Bigstock.com, p. 20 (middle); © Yastremska/Bigstock.com, pp. 20 (right top), 25 (bottom right); © Mates/Bigstock.com, p. 21 (top); © Liveshot/ Bigstock.com, p. 21 (center); © iStockphoto.com/John Shepherd, p. 22 (bottom); © Billyfoto/Bigstock.com, p. 22 (top); © Ew Ilkerson/Dreamstime.com, p. 23 (bottom middle); © Lija Generalov/Shutterstock.com, p. 23 (bottom right); © Ragnarock/Bigstock.com, p. 23 (bottom left); p. 25 (top); © iStockphoto.com/dendong, p. 23 (top middle); © iStockphoto.com/Evgenia Bolyukh, p. 24 (top); © iStockphoto.com/Keilchi Hiki, p. 24 (bottom left); © Nata Sha/ Shutterstock.com, p. 24 (bottom middle); © LittleStocker/Shutterstock.com, p. 25 (middle); © Helen Sessions/Alamy, p. 25 (bottom left); © Rony Zmiri/Bigstock.com, p. 26; © iStockphoto.com/Warren Price, p. 28 (top left); © iStockphoto. com/Руслан Кудрин, p. 28 (bottom left); © iStockphoto.com/Antagain, p. 28 (bottom right); © Vvoevale/Dreamstime. com, p. 28 (top right); © Jian Zhang/Dreamstime.com, p. 29 (top); © Maryloo/Bigstock.com, p. 29 (bottom right); © Elnur/Bigstock.com, pp. 30 (top left), 30 (top right), 30 (bottom left); © iStockphoto.com/Felinda, p. 31 (middle right); © Angie/Bigstock.com, pp. 31 (top), 38 (bottom); © shippee, p. 31 (middle left); © iStockphoto.com/Natallia Bokach, p. 31 (bottom); © iStockphoto.com/zxvisual, p. 32 (top right); © Postolit/Dreamstime.com, p. 32 (bottom right); © Abracadabra99/Bigstock.com, p. 32 (top left); © Aaron Amat/Bigstock.com, p. 33 (bottom left); © Frazer Harrison/ Getty Images, p. 33 (bottom right); © Photocell/Shutterstock.com, p. 34; © iStockphoto.com/WEKWEK, p. 36 (top); © iStockphoto.com/High Impact Photography, p. 36 (middle top); © Kuleczka/Bigstock.com, p. 36 (middle bottom); © iStockphoto.com/Jean Assell, p. 36 (bottom); © iStockphoto.com/iconogenic, p. 37 (inset); © Jupiter Images/Polka Dot/Getty Images/Thinkstock, p. 37; © Massimo Merlini/E+/Getty Images, p. 38 (top); © iStockphoto.com/Oleg Filipchuk, p. 39 (bottom); © Milosluz/Bigstock.com, p. 39 (top); © iStockphoto.com/Jennifer Duncan, p. 40; © Nata Sha/ Shutterstock.com, p. 43 (bottom); © iStockphoto.com/somkcr, p. 44 (top); © iStockphoto.com/EHStock, p. 44 (bottom).

Backgrounds: © NannaDesign/Bigstock.com, pp. 1, 4–5, 20–21; © Jodielee/Dreamstime.com, pp. 6, 14–15, 16, 42–43, 44–45; © Daniana/Shutterstock.com, pp. 9, 10–11, 12, 46–47, 48; © Cherry Blossom Girl/Bigstock.com, p. 16, 19, 24, 28, 36 © iStockphoto.com/amdandy, p. 18; © smilewithjul/Bigstock.com, p. 30; © Marussia/Shutterstock.com, p. 38; © Annareichel/Shutterstock.com, p. 39.

Front cover: © Milosluz/Bigstock.com (feather); © RuslanOmega/Bigstock.com (earrings); © ppart/Shutterstock. com (leather bag); © Lija Generalov/Shutterstock.com (shoes); © Ragnarock/Shutterstock.com (boots); © Karkas/ Bigstock.com (blouse), (skirt); © iStockphoto/Thinkstock (belt); © Khz/Dreamstime.com (daisy); © Abracadabra99/ Bigstock.com (hat); © NannaDesign/Bigstock.com (background).

Back cover: © Aaron Amat/Bigstock.com (sunglasses); © Fibobjects/Dreamstime.com (daisy); © Cristi180884/ Bigstock.com (sandals); © iStockphoto.com/penguenstok (cardigan); © amdandy, (background).